Food From Another Country

Wil Spencer

Each of these foods was first made in another country.

Have you ever eaten **pizza**? Pizza was first made in another country.

Now people make pizza here.

Have you ever eaten **sushi**? Sushi was first made in another country.

Now people make sushi here.

Have you ever eaten a **taco**? **Tacos** were first made in another country.

Now people make tacos here.

Have you ever eaten a **shish kebab**? **Shish kebabs** were first made in another country.

Now people make **shish kebabs** here.

What is your favorite food from another country?